Tempting and Tasty

GW00705952

Recipes to make, taste and enjoy!!

ISBN: 0-9550597-0-4

Published by

© **Tulla Crafts**

Based in The Glens of Antrim

web: **www.tullacrafts.com**

email: **twospoiltboxers@btinternet.com**

© Photographs McCaughan 2005 all rights reserved

designed by The Universities Press (Belfast) Ltd.
printed by BookPublishingWorld.
edited by Impact Printing & Publishing.

Reprint 2007

The Nine Glens

There are nine glens in Antrim,
Nine great glens in all,
Glenarm is the first one,
And near Cushendall
There's lovely Glenariff,
Glenaan and Glendun,
And nestling between them
Glenballyeamon.
Glencorp and Glenshesk,
Come on, don't be lazy,
There is only Glencloy,
And the last one, Glentaisie.

From: "By Winding Roads"
By John Irvine

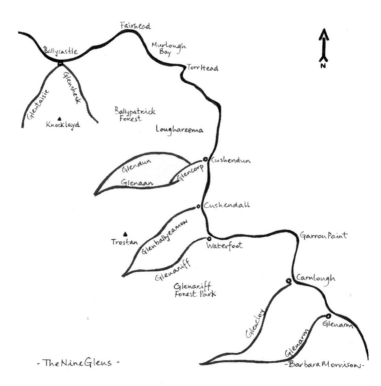

— The Nine Glens —

—Barbara Morrison—

The Nine Glens of Antrim

Glenarm: *Gleann Arma*   The glen of the army

Glencloy: *Gleann Claidhe*   The glen of the hedges

Glenariff: *Gleann Airimh*   The arable or fertile glen

Glenballyeamon: *Gleann Bhaile Eamoinn* Edwardstown glen

Glenaan: *Gleann Adhann*   The glen of the colt's foot

Glencorp: *Gleann Coirp*   The glen of the slaughtered

Glendun: *Gleann Abhain Doinne*   The glen of the brown river

Glenshesk: *Gleann Seist*   The glen of the sedges

Glentaise: *Gleann Taoise Taobh Geal*   The glen of Princess Taise

Table of Oven Temperatures

Approximate Circotherm Equivalent (°C)	Conventional Electric Oven (°F)	Conventional Electric Oven (°C)	Conventional Gas Mark
100	200	100	1/4
110	225	110	1/4
120	250	130	1/2
130	275	140	1
140	300	150	2
150	325	160-170	3
160	350-375	180-190	4-5
170	400	200	6
180	425	220	7
190	450-500	230-240	8-9

Table of Equivalents

Imperial	Metric
1 oz	25g
2 oz	50g
3 oz	75g
4 oz	100g
5 oz	125g
6 oz	155g
7 oz	175g
8 oz	200g
1/4 pint or 5 fluid oz	150ml Approx.
1/2 pint or 10 fluid oz	275ml Approx.
3/4 pint or 15 fluid oz	425ml Approx.
1 pint or 20 fluid oz	570ml Approx.
1 1/4 pint or 25 fluid oz	700ml Approx.
1 1/2 pint or 30 fluid oz	850ml Approx.
1 teaspoon (tsp)	5ml
1 dessertspoon (dsp)	10ml
1 tablespoon (tbsp)	15ml

Soups

Main Courses

Hot and Cold Desserts

Cakes and Tray Bakes

Bread and Scones

Drinks

Giants Causeway

by permission of The National Trust

Soups

He who does not get meat thinks soup a great luxury.
An té ná faghann an fheóil is mór an sógh leis an t-anairthe.

Tomato Soup

(Serves 4 - 6)

INGREDIENTS

400g ripe tomatoes
1 large onion
1 large carrot
1 stick of celery
2 rashers back bacon
25g butter
600ml water

Seasoning - salt + pepper
A few bay leaves
Parsley sprigs
5 ml mixed herbs
5 ml thyme
5 ml sage
3 - 4 whole cloves
} **Bouquet Garnet**

Small tin of cream of tomato soup - for colour
Finely chopped parsley to garnish.

METHOD

1. Skin and chop the tomatoes.

2. Chop the onion.

3. Wash, peel, and grate the carrot.

4. Wash and chop celery.

5. Remove the rind and fat from the bacon and cut into small pieces using kitchen scissors.

6. Melt the butter; toss the bacon in the melted butter.

7. Add the vegetables and toss again but do not brown.

8. Add the water, seasoning and Bouquet Garni.

9. Cover and simmer gently for 35 minutes approx.

10. Taste, adjust seasoning, liquidise, and stir in can of tomato soup.

11. Reheat before serving piping hot and sprinkle with chopped parsley.

Cream of Mushroom Soup

(Serves 3)

INGREDIENTS

25g block margarine
25g plain flour
250ml chicken stock
250ml milk
1 x 15ml lemon juice
2 x 15ml thick cream
100-200g mushrooms,
washed and finely chopped
Seasoning

TO SERVE:

Chopped parsley
1 x 15ml thick cream

METHOD

1. Place all the ingredients for the soup in a large saucepan except lemon juice and cream.

2. Whisk continuously over a moderate heat; bring to the boil, lower heat.

3. Cover and simmer for 10 minutes.

4. Remove soup from heat; add lemon juice and cream.

5. Serve sprinkled with chopped parsley and a swirl of cream.

Vegetable Soup

(Serves 4-6)

INGREDIENTS

25g block margarine
50g bacon, chopped
1 small onion, chopped
$^1/_2$ stick celery, chopped
1 carrot, diced
1 clove garlic, crushed (optional)
1 vegetable stock cube
1 litre hot water
25g crushed vermicelli
1 slice cooked ham cut into squares
Fresh parsley, chopped

METHOD

1. Melt margarine in large saucepan and fry bacon, onion, celery, carrot and garlic (if used) for 5 minutes.

2. Dissolve stock cube in hot water and add to saucepan.

3. Bring to boil, simmer for 10 minutes.

4. Add crushed vermicelli and ham to the soup.

5. Cook for another 5 minutes.

6. Sprinkle with parsley before serving.

Serving suggestion - serve with wheaten bread.

Onion, Potato and Leek Soup

(Serves 4)

INGREDIENTS

4 large leeks
4 large potatoes, peeled and diced
2 medium onions, finely chopped
50g block margarine
600ml vegetable stock (use 2 stock cubes)
200ml semi-skimmed milk
Seasoning

TO SERVE:

Fresh chopped parsley

METHOD

1. Prepare leeks: trim the tops and roots. Discard tough outer leaves and slit in half lengthways. Slice finely and rinse thoroughly in a colander. Drain well.

2. In a large saucepan melt margarine, add leeks, potatoes and onions, stirring them all thoroughly. Season well, cover and let the vegetables sweat* over a low heat for 10 - 15 minutes.

3. Add stock and milk, bring to simmering** point and with lid on, simmer for 20 minutes or until the vegetables are tender. Do not boil or milk will boil over.

4. Place soup in a blender and puree to desired consistency. Return to the saucepan and reheat gently. Check seasoning. Serve sprinkled with parsley.

*To sweat - coats the vegetables with fat and draws out their juices and flavours.

** Simmering - slight quivering of liquid just before it comes to the boil.

Pumpkin Soup

(Serves 6-8)

INGREDIENTS

1 x 15ml cooking oil
25g butter
1 onion, chopped
3 carrots, chopped
2 potatoes, chopped
375g pumpkin flesh
Seasoning
900ml vegetable stock
(2 vegetable stock cubes)

METHOD

1. Heat the oil and butter in a large saucepan, add the onion and fry until softened (about 5 minutes). Do not brown onion.

2. Add the remaining vegetables and stir well.

3. Add salt, pepper and the stock. Bring to the boil.

4. Cover and simmer for 30 minutes, until the vegetables are tender.

5. Puree, then return to the pan, reheat before serving.

Potato Soup

(Serves 4)

INGREDIENTS

1 vegetable stock cube
500ml water
3 small potatoes
1 small carrot
1 small onion
50ml milk
Seasoning

TO SERVE:

Fresh chopped parsley

METHOD

1. Peel and slice potatoes. Grate carrot. Chop onion.

2. Dissolve stock cube in water, add seasoning and vegetables and simmer for 20-25 minutes in a saucepan.

3. Liquidise in blender or processor. Return to saucepan.

4. Add milk and reheat.

5. Serve hot, sprinkled with finely chopped parsley.

Cream of Cauliflower Soup

(Serves 4)

INGREDIENTS

1 medium sized onion, peeled and chopped
2 potatoes, peeled and chopped
1 head of cauliflower, divided into florets
2 sticks celery, chopped
500ml vegetable stock (use 1 vegetable stock cube)
Seasoning
Grated cheese to serve

METHOD

1. Melt the butter in a large saucepan. Add the prepared vegetables and cook over a gentle heat for 5 minutes.

2. Add stock, stir, cover and bring to the boil.

3. Simmer for 20 minutes until the vegetables are tender.

4. Liquidise the soup and return to the saucepan.

5. Stir in cream and reheat soup. Do not allow to boil.

6. Season to taste.

7. Sprinkle grated cheese on top and serve hot.

Broth

(Serves 3-4)

INGREDIENTS

1 shank of lamb
600ml water
1 lamb stock cube
1 packet prepared soup
vegetable (wash)
2 x 15ml barley

TO SERVE:

chopped parsley

METHOD

1. Put shank of lamb in a medium sized saucepan. Cover with water, bring to the boil. A scum will form. Remove from heat.

2. Lift shank out of water, discard water and rinse out saucepan.

3. Return shank to saucepan cover with 600ml of fresh water. Add stock cube, bring to the boil and simmer for 1^1/$_2$ hours.

4. When meat is cooked remove from saucepan, trim the meat off the bone and cut into pieces.

5. Skim any fat off stock in saucepan, return the pieces of meat to the saucepan.

6. Add the soup vegetables.

7. Bring to the boil, reduce heat and simmer for an hour. Sprinkle with chopped parsley before serving.

Main Courses

May good luck be your friend in whatever you do,
And may trouble be always a stranger to you.

Shepherd's Pie

(Serves 4)

INGREDIENTS

500g cooked minced lamb (fry in own fat until well browned)
3 carrots washed and peeled
2 small onions
1.5kg mashed potatoes
300ml lamb stock (use 1 lamb stock cube and 300ml boiling water)
Parsley to garnish
100g butter

METHOD

1. Wash, peel and boil potatoes until soft.

2. Place a layer of mincemeat in a pie dish.

3. Cover with a layer of onions.

4. Place a layer of carrots on top.

5. Make up a lamb stock.

6. Pour it over the meat, onion and carrots.

7. Mash potatoes and use to cover the meat, onions and carrots.

8. Use a knife to make a pattern on the top of the potatoes, cover with pats of butter at 150°C/325°F/Gas 3 for 1 hour.

Brown Stew

(Serves 4)

INGREDIENTS

400g stewing steak
100g seasoned flour (flour with salt and pepper added)
1 onion
15ml cooking oil
2 carrots
1 small turnip
600ml beef stock
50g cornflour
2.5ml teaspoon gravy browning } *thickening

METHOD

1. Cut the meat into square pieces and toss in seasoned flour.

2. Peel and slice the onion.

3. Warm the oil in a thick-bottomed saucepan. When hot fry both the meat and onion until well browned.

4. Add carrot, turnip and sufficient stock to cover all.

5. Bring to the boil, simmer gently for 2 hours or until meat is tender.

6. Thicken just before transferring into a warmed casserole dish for serving.

To thicken place cornflour in a small bowl, stir in some of the liquid from the stew to make a paste, add gravy browning. Slowly add to the stew, stirring constantly to prevent lumps forming.

Meat Loaf

(Serves 4-6)

INGREDIENTS
500g lean minced beef
60g brown breadcrumbs
1 small onion, chopped
10ml mixed herbs
1 clove of garlic
2.5ml salt
2.5 pepper

METHOD
1. Mix the mince and breadcrumbs together.

2. Add the onion, mixed herbs, crushed garlic, salt and pepper to the meat mixture.

3. Place in a 17cm x 7.5cm x 6cm loaf tin lined with a loaf tin liner (1lb). Cover with foil.

4. Bake at 160°C/350°F/Gas 4 for 1 -1^1/2hours.

5. Serve hot with tomato sauce and mashed potatoes or serve cold, sliced with salad.

TOMATO SAUCE

INGREDIENTS
1 onion chopped
A little oil for frying
45g flour
250ml tomato juice
250ml veg. stock (use vegetable stock cube)
1 bay leaf
2.5ml sugar
Salt and pepper to taste

METHOD
1. Finely chop onion and fry in a little oil.
2. Stir in flour, slowly.
3. Gradually add the tomato juice and vegetable stock.
4. Add bay leaf, sugar, salt and pepper to taste.
5. Bring to the boil, stirring continuously and then simmer for ^{1}/2 hour.
6. Strain before pouring sauce over hot meat loaf.

Sirloins in Foil

(Serves 4)

INGREDIENTS

4 x 200g Sirloin steaks
100g mushrooms
1 medium onion
4 medium tomatoes
Salt and pepper to taste
1 x 10ml oil for frying
Chopped parsley to garnish

METHOD

1. Cut 4 squares of tinfoil, large enough to wrap around each steak.

2. Chop mushrooms, onion and tomatoes finely.

3. Heat oil in a fairly large frying pan over a high heat, fry the steaks for 1 minute per side.

4. Place each steak on a square of tinfoil.

5. Place mushrooms, onion and tomatoes in the pan in which the steaks were browned and fry until brown.

6. Divide this mixture over the top of each steak, season and close up the tinfoil to make 4 individual parcels.

7. Place steak parcels on a baking sheet and complete the cooking in a moderate oven 160°C/350°F/Gas 4-5.

Cooking time:
Under done 15 minutes.

Well done   30 minutes.

8. Sprinkle with chopped parsley and serve with oven chips or creamed potatoes and vegetables of your choice.

Steak Diane

(Serves 4)

INGREDIENTS

4 x 200g sirloin steaks
1 onion
2 x 5ml caster sugar
1 medium lemon
100g unsalted butter
Worcestershire sauce
1 x 15ml chopped parsley
3 x 15ml Brandy

METHOD

1. Trim the steaks and beat them flat with a rolling pin until they are no more than 8mm thick.

2. Peel and finely chop the onion.

3. Grate the lemon rind finely, squeeze out the juice and strain.

4. Melt 50g of the butter in a large, heavy-based pan and fry the onion for about 5 minutes, or until soft and transparent.

5. Lift the onion on to a plate with a perforated spoon and keep warm.

6. Fry two steaks at a time (depending on size), over a high heat (for 1 minute only) on each side.

7. Lift out and keep warm.

8. Melt another 50g of butter until foaming.

9. Fry 2 more steaks.

10. Return the onions to the pan, stir in the sugar, lemon rind and juice, add about six drops of Worcestershire sauce and the parsley.

11. Cook gently for a few minutes. Then add the steaks and Brandy. *Flambé them.

12. Serve the steaks with the onion and sauce from the frying pan poured over them.

SERVING SUGGESTION:

New potatoes and braised celery are suitable vegetables

*flambé: to cook food in flaming Brandy.

Beef Cobbler

FOR 6 PORTIONS:
500 - 600g stewing steak
75g flour
Seasoning (salt + pepper)
50g fat
2 onions
Whole baby carrots
Few frozen or fresh peas
(optional)
2 sliced tomatoes
12 small potatoes
600ml brown stock or water and
stock cubes

COBBLER PASTRY:
150g self-raising flour
5ml baking powder
Pinch salt
50g margarine
Milk to mix

TO GARNISH:
Chopped parsley.

TO SERVE:
Garnish the cobbler scones with
chopped parsley, and serve with
a green vegetable.

TO VARY:
Other meats may be topped in
this way or the cobbler pastry
(scone like pastry) put on top of
fruit.

METHOD
1. Prepare the steak - cut into
    neat pieces.

2. Roll in the seasoned flour
    and fry in the hot fat for a
    few minutes in a large
    saucepan.

3. Add the onions and carrots
    and cook in the fat for 2 - 3
    minutes.

4. Gradually stir in the stock,
    bring to the boil, cook until
    the sauce has thickened -
    lower the heat and simmer
    for 1 hour.

5. Add the peas, tomatoes and
    potatoes, cook for a further
    $^1/2$ hour.

6. Transfer to a casserole, top
    with the rounds of cobbler
    pastry and bake until
    golden brown. Put a piece
    of foil over the meat, which
    has been left exposed, to
    prevent drying.

TO MAKE THE COBBLER PASTRY:
Sieve flour, baking powder and
salt, rub in margarine, bind with
milk. Roll out to 1cm thick, cut
in rounds and use as required.

Stir Fry Chicken

(Serves 4)

INGREDIENTS

4 chicken fillets
1 clove garlic (crushed)
200g broccoli
1 onion
2 x 20ml cornflour
8 x 20ml chicken stock
A little vegetable oil
100g mushrooms
1 large carrot
100g bean sprouts (optional)
4 x 2ml Soya sauce
Seasoning

METHOD

1. Cut chicken into strips. Peel and chop onion and garlic. Wash and slice mushrooms. Cut into slices.

2. Place cooking oil in a pan or Wok and heat over a high heat. Add garlic and onion and cook for 1 minute (approximately). Add chicken strips and fry for 3 - 4 minutes. Remove from pan.

3. Stir-fry broccoli, mushrooms, carrots and bean sprouts for 3 - 4 minutes.

4. Blend chicken stock, Soya sauce and cornflour in a small bowl. Season well. Return chicken and onion to pan containing the vegetables and add liquid. Cover and cook for 2 - 3 minutes and serve hot.

Serving Suggestion:
Serve hot with garlic bread or wheaten bread.

Hawaiian Chicken

(Serves 2-3)

INGREDIENTS

25g margarine
1 onion
1 green pepper
25g flour
250ml chicken stock
200g cooked chicken
200g pineapple cubes
Salt and pepper
175g sweetcorn (frozen or tinned)
200g long grain rice
125g whipping cream

TO SERVE:

Garnish with chopped parsley

METHOD

1. Cook rice in boiling salted water for 20 minutes approx.

2. Peel and chop the onion.

3. Remove the stalk and seeds from the green pepper and chop finely.

4. Melt the margarine and fry the onion and pepper.

5. Stir in the flour and gradually add the stock

6. Bring to the boil and cook for 1 minute.

7. Add pineapples, chicken and seasoning. Heat thoroughly.

8. Just before the rice finishes cooking, add sweetcorn, then after 2 minutes drain carefully.

9. Arrange rice on serving dish in a ring.

10. Add cream to chicken sauce and carefully pour the chicken inside the ring of rice.

Sweet and Sour Pork

(Serves 5)

INGREDIENTS

300g pork pieces
1 small tin crushed pineapple
1 small onion, chopped
1 x 10ml vinegar
1 x 10ml concentrated tomato puree
3 x 20ml brown sugar
1 x 5ml Soya sauce
100g mushrooms, washed and sliced
1 large carrot, washed and peeled (cut into long very thin strips)

METHOD

1. Prepare all ingredients. Remember to soak rice for 1hr at this stage (see instructions for Jasmine Rice).

2. Stew* the pork in a saucepan with the crushed pineapple (and the juice) for 5 minutes.

3. Add all the other ingredients and simmer for 40 minutes.

4. The sauce should not be too watery - if necessary thicken with a little blended cornflour.

5. Serve with boiled rice. Allow 60g of rice per person.

JASMINE RICE IS LIGHTER AND FLUFFIER THAN BASMATI RICE

1. Weigh out required amount (allow 60g per person) and soak in cold water for 1 hour.

2. Drain, add the rice to a large saucepan of boiling water.

3. Partly cook for 5 minutes ONLY.

4. Drain, place in steamer.

5. Set over simmering water for 15 minutes.

6. The rice will be tender and separated.

7. Make sure there is water in the steamer, put the heat to low to keep rice hot for up to an hour.

To stew - cook in a small, measured amount of liquid which is only allowed to simmer, This liquid is always served with the food.

Baked Stuffed Sausages

(Serves 3)

INGREDIENTS

6 sausages
6 slices of bacon
60g of breadcrumbs
1 small onion finely chopped
Salt and pepper to season
A little milk or yolk of egg to blend

METHOD

1. Slit the sausages up the centre.

2. Mix all the ingredients for stuffing together, blend with milk or egg yolk.

3. Place some stuffing along the open slit in the sausage.

4. Remove rind from bacon and wrap bacon round sausage, secure with wooden cocktail sticks.

5. Place on a baking sheet with a rim round it.

6. Bake towards the top of the oven at 170°C/400°F/Gas 6 for 30 minutes. Or until nicely browned.

7. Remove from the oven, take out cocktail sticks.

8. Arrange attractively on a dish, garnish with parsley and serve.

May you live as long as you want
And never want as long as you live

Spaghetti Bolognese

(Serves 2-3)

INGREDIENTS

150g mince steak

1 small onion

1 clove garlic

25g mushrooms (optional)

1 stick celery

1 small carrot

1 small tin of tomatoes

1 x 10ml tomato puree

Pinch of mixed herbs

Black pepper

2 x 5ml oil

$1/2$ beef stock cube dissolved in 50ml water

150g Spaghetti (fresh or dried)

TO SERVE:

Grated Parmesan cheese.

METHOD

1. Crush garlic using a garlic crusher.

2. Chop the onion, grate the carrot, chop mushrooms and celery finely.

3. Heat the oil in a saucepan and gently fry the onion and garlic.

4. Increase the heat, add the meat and brown. Drain off any excess fat.

5. Add all the other sauce ingredients and simmer for 20-30 minutes.

6. Cook the spaghetti in boiling salted water as directed on the packet. Drain well.

7. To serve, arrange spaghetti round edge of a deep dish, pour meat sauce in the middle and serve sprinkled with a little Parmesan cheese.

Honey, Mustard and Sugar Glazed Ham

INGREDIENTS

1 smoked half gammon with bone in (4 kg approx.)
1 large onion, peeled and studded with a few cloves
A few bay leaves
2 litres of dry cider
Cold water to cover the ham
Whole black peppercorns

Glaze

6 x 15ml prepared Dijon Mustard
6 x 15ml honey
6 x 15ml demerara sugar
6 x 15ml soft brown sugar
Cloves to stud
500ml cider to bake

METHOD

1. Soak the ham overnight in cold water with a few bay leaves.

2. Next day wash under cold running water.

3. Place the ham in a large saucepan that it fits into comfortably and cover with cold water.

4. Add an onion studded with cloves, cider, peppercorns and bay leaves.

5. Bring to the boil and simmer gently for $2^1/2$ hours.

6. Remove the ham and cool slightly, then, using a sharp knife, score the fat diagonally, first in one direction then the other, creating a diamond-shaped pattern.

7. Mix the mustard and honey together and, using either your hands or a flat-bladed knife, spread the mixture over the top of the ham.

8. Stud each diamond shape with a clove, and sprinkle with brown sugar, patting down well.

9. Line a roasting tin with tinfoil. Pour 500ml cider into the roasting tin. Transfer the ham into this tin.

10. Bake for the 2 hours 160°C/350°F/Gas 5 basting occasionally. Remove or open up tinfoil 20-30 mins before the end of the cooking time to allow the ham to brown.

Tagliatelle Alla Carbonara

(Serves 3-4)

INGREDIENTS

400g Tagliatelle
Seasoning
6 rashers back bacon diced
25g butter
2 medium eggs, lightly beaten
150ml single cream
1 clove garlic crushed
(optional)
25 - 50g mushrooms
(optional)
1 small onion finely chopped
Chopped parsley
50g Parmesan cheese, grated

METHOD

1. Cook the Tagliatelle in a large saucepan of boiling salted water for 10 - 15 minutes until just tender.

2. Drain and place in a serving dish, keep warm.

3. Fry the bacon in the butter (until crispy) along with the onion, garlic and mushrooms.

4. Reduce the heat, add the eggs, cream and parsley. Season to taste.

5. Add half the Parmesan cheese and heat gently without boiling. Stir continuously.

6. Pour the sauce over the Tagliatelle, then sprinkle the remaining Parmesan cheese on top and serve immediately.

Vegetable Risotto

(Serves 1-2)

INGREDIENTS

75g long grain rice
1 x 15ml cooking oil
15g margarine
$^1/_4$ onion, chopped
$^1/_2$ garlic clove, crushed
300ml water
1 vegetable stock cube
$^1/_2$ tomato, chopped
10ml turmeric (a yellow spice)
15g peas, frozen
15g sweetcorn, frozen
25g mushrooms, washed and sliced
$^1/_4$ stick celery washed + sliced
$^1/_4$ courgette washed + sliced
$^1/_4$ red pepper washed + sliced

TO SERVE:

Grated Cheddar cheese.

METHOD

1. Place stock cube and turmeric in a measuring jug and make up to 300ml with boiling water.

2. Heat the oil and margarine in a saucepan. Add the onion and garlic and fry gently for a few minutes.

3. Add the rice to the onion and garlic and stir well until mixed.

4. Add all the remaining vegetables and stir gently over the heat for 3 - 4 minutes.

5. Add the stock mixture. Bring to the boil and simmer gently.

6. When the rice and vegetables are tender and most of the liquid has been absorbed (15-20 minutes), remove from the heat.

7. Turn out onto a heated dish and sprinkle with grated Cheddar cheese.

Quick Cheese Pizza

(Serves 3-4)

INGREDIENTS

SCONE BASE
50g flora margarine
25g wholemeal flour
200g self-raising flour
1 x 15ml mixed herbs
4 x 15ml milk approx
1 large egg
TOPPING
3 slices rindless bacon (cut into small pieces)
1 small onion (chopped)
50g mushrooms (sliced)
230g tin chopped tomatoes
1 x 5ml mixed herbs
200g Cheddar cheese (grated)

Optional:
red/green pepper for garnish

METHOD

1. Pre-heat oven 180°C/425°F/Gas 7.

2. Mix ALL scone ingredients together in a bowl using a fork.

3. Knead lightly and then press into a 25.5cm greased pizza plate.

4. CAREFULLY fry the bacon in its own fat, add chopped onion and sliced mushrooms.

5. Add tin of chopped tomatoes and mixed herbs, *reduce. Spread over the base.

6. Sprinkle with cheese and decorate with peppers.

7. Bake in pre-heated oven for 20 minutes approx.

Reduce means to allow some of the liquid to boil off therefore reducing the amount of liquid and thickening the sauce.

Lasagne

(Serves 2-3)

INGREDIENTS

4 - 6 sheets of Lasagne pasta
(pre-cooked)

MEAT SAUCE

200g minced beef
1 medium onion
10ml vegetable oil
1 small can tomatoes chopped
1 x 5ml tomato puree
Pinch of mixed herbs

CHEESE SAUCE

275ml milk
25g block margarine
25g plain flour
1 x 5ml mustard
75g grated cheese

METHOD

1. Pre-heat oven to

    170°C /400°F/Gas 6.

2. Peel and chop onion.

3. Heat oil in pan, cook
    onion for 1 - 2 minutes.

4. Add meat and cook until
    browned.

5. Add can of tomatoes,
    tomato puree and herbs.
    Simmer.

6. Make the cheese sauce (all
    in one method): put the
    milk, flour, margarine and
    mustard into a saucepan.
    Bring to the boil, whisking
    all the time until
    thickened. Add most of the
    grated cheese (save a little
    for the top). Season if
    necessary.

7. Put layers of cheese sauce,
    lasagne and meat into a
    small ovenproof dish.
    Finish with a layer of
    cheese sauce.

8. Sprinkle with the
    remaining cheese.

9. Place on a baking tray in
    the centre of the oven for
    about 20 - 30 minutes
    until golden brown.

SERVE WITH:

Green salad and Garlic bread.

Quiche Lorraine

(Serves 4)

INGREDIENTS

150g plain flour
75g margarine
Pinch of salt
Water to mix

Rub fat into flour with fingertips. Add a pinch of salt and enough water to bind

FILLING:

1 small onion
2 rashers streaky bacon
12g margarine for frying
3 - 4 egg yolks
75ml milk
Salt and pepper
75g grated cheddar cheese
Parsley to garnish

METHOD

1. Make the pastry, roll out and use to line a 17cm greased sandwich tin or flan ring.

2. Chop the onion very finely and cut the bacon into small squares.

3. Fry the bacon and onion gently in the margarine until both are quite tender, turn them into the pastry case.

4. Beat the eggs and milk, stir in the seasoning and most of the cheese.

5. Pour this mixture into the case and sprinkle the top with the rest of the cheese.

6. Bake for 10 minutes, then reduce oven to 160°C/350°F/Gas 5 and bake for a further 30 minutes.

7. Garnish with parsley.

Pacific Pie and Potato Wedges

(Serves 2)

PACIFIC PIE
INGREDIENTS

- 200g tin tuna
- 1 small tin condensed chicken soup
- 50g sweetcorn
- 50g garden peas
- 1 packet ready salted crisps
- 25g low fat cheddar cheese

METHOD

1. Pre-heat oven 170°C/400°F/Gas 6.
2. Wipe the lid of the tuna tin and open.
3. Flake the fish with a fork and place in a pie dish.
4. Cover with the sweetcorn and peas.
5. Pour the soup over the mixture.
6. Crush the crisps in the bag before opening and sprinkle over the soup
7. Cover with the grated cheese and place oven-proof dish in the pre-heated oven.
8. Bake for 30 minutes or place in a microwave for 5 minutes and brown under a grill if necessary.

POTATO WEDGES
INGREDIENTS

- 2 large potatoes
- 1 x 15ml cooking oil

METHOD

1. Pre-heat oven 170°C/400°F/Gas 6.
2. Scrub the potatoes and dry.
3. Cut into 8 long wedge shapes and place in a bowl along with the oil. Make sure the wedges are completely coated in oil.
4. Spread the wedges out on a baking tray.
5. Place in the oven and cook until tender and brown. Turn halfway through cooking time (approx. 30 minutes.).

Tinned Salmon can be used instead of the Tuna.

Fish Crumble

(Serves 2)

FILLING
200g cod
25g margarine
15g plain flour
125ml milk
1 x 15ml lemon juice

TOPPING
50g plain flour
25g margarine
50g grated Cheddar cheese

GARNISH
chopped parsley

METHOD

1. Pre-heat oven to 160°C/350°F/Gas 5.

2. Lightly grease a small ovenproof dish.

3. Cut the fish into small pieces and place in the serving dish.

4. Place the margarine, flour and milk in a small saucepan.

5. Heat over a gentle heat until thick, whisking continuously with a balloon whisk.

6. Add lemon juice and pour over fish.

8. To make topping, rub margarine into flour until mixture resembles fine breadcrumbs.

9. Mix in cheese, spread this topping over the fish mixture.

10. Bake in the preheated oven for 25 minutes.

11. Serve sprinkled with chopped parsley.

Cold and Hot Desserts

The proof of the pudding lies in the eating of it.
I n-ithe na potóige bhíonn a tástáil.

Pineapple Upside Down Pudding

(Serves 4-5)

INGREDIENTS
5 pineapple rings
1 x 15ml golden syrup
3 glacé cherries for the centre of
the pineapple rings.

SPONGE:
100g Margarine
100g caster sugar
100g plain flour
1 x 5ml baking powder
2 eggs
15ml boiling water - depends on
size of eggs.

SAUCE:
25g Flour
2 x 15ml sugar
Knob of butter or margarine
300ml pineapple juice and water

METHOD
1. Pre-heat oven
   160°C/350°F/Gas 5. Grease
   an 18cm round cake tin,
   line the centre with greased
   greaseproof paper.
2. Open the tin of pineapples
   and strain.
3. Arrange the pineapple rings
   on the base of the cake tin.
4. Cut the cherries in half and
   put in the centre of the
   pineapple rings.
5. Heat the syrup gently and
   pour over the fruit.
6. Cream fat and sugar.
7. Gradually beat in the eggs.
8. Gradually sieve and fold in
   the flour.
9. Place spoonfuls of the cake
   mixture evenly over the
   fruit, starting from the
   outside of the tin and
   working inwards.
10. Level surface of cake with a
    knife.
11. Bake in the centre of the
    oven for 30-40 minutes or
    until well-risen, golden and
    firm to touch.
12. Turn onto a serving plate,
    shaking gently to loosen
    pudding.
13. Serve pudding with the
    pineapple sauce.

PINEAPPLE SAUCE
1. Melt the margarine.
2. Stir in the sugar and flour,
   gradually add the juice and
   water
3. Allow to thicken slightly
   before pouring into a
   sauceboat.

Steamed Peaches with Cointreau

(Serves 4)

INGREDIENTS
4 peaches (or apricots)
Small block of vanilla ice cream

SAUCE:
Juice of $1/2$ orange
Juice of $1/2$ lemon
15ml caster sugar
150ml double cream
15ml of Cointreau
Chocolate vermicelli

METHOD
1. *Steam the number of peaches required until soft (about 10-15 minutes).

2. Allow to cool slightly but while still warm remove the stone and the skin from the peaches.

3. Cool completely before filling with ice cream.

FOR THE SAUCE:
Whip the juice, sugar and cream until creamy and thick.
Fold in the Cointreau and pour over the peaches, decorate with a little chocolate vermicelli.

---

* To steam is to cook food in the steam from rapidly boiling water.

Sponge Pudding

(Serves 1-2)

INGREDIENTS

50g margarine
50g caster sugar
50g self-raising flour
1 egg
10ml almond essence
Peach or pear slices

METHOD

1. Light the oven, 160°C/350°F/Gas 5.

2. Arrange slices of fruit on the base of a small foil dish, 141mm x 116mm x 41mm.

3. Beat margarine and sugar together with a wooden spoon until light and fluffy or use hand-held electric whisk. Add the egg. Sieve the flour and add to mixture. Add almond essence. Mix thoroughly.

4. Spread this mixture carefully over the fruit.

5. Bake for about 30 minutes until firm.

SERVE WITH:

custard/cream.

Apple Tart

(Serves 4-6)

INGREDIENTS
125g self-raising flour
150g plain flour
125g block margarine
45ml cold water approx.
2 large cooking apples
A little sugar
Ground cloves
Ground cinnamon
A little beaten egg (to glaze)

METHOD
1. Turn on oven
   160°C/350°F/Gas 5.

2. Either use a food processor to make the pastry or sieve the flour into a baking bowl and rub in the margarine using the fingertips until the mixture resembles fine breadcrumbs.

3. Bind the pastry together with the cold water.

4. If time allows, "relax" the pastry in the fridge to prevent shrinkage for 30 mins.

5. Grease a 20cm tinfoil pie plate using margarine paper.

6. Divide the pastry into two thirds and one third.

7. Roll out two-thirds pastry and use to line greased pie plate.

8. Trim and dampen edges.

9. Wash, peel, quarter and core apples, work quickly to prevent browning.

10. Slice the apples on top of the pastry, sprinkle with sugar, cloves and cinnamon.

11. Cover the apples with the remaining pastry. Trim. Seal the edges of the pastry by pressing down with the back of a spoon handle. Cut a slit in top of the tart.

12. Glaze with beaten egg. Bake for 30-40 minutes.

13. Dredge with caster sugar when tart is removed from

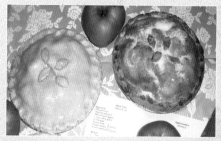

Rhubarb Crumble

(Serves 4-5)

INGREDIENTS

400g rhubarb sticks, wipe with damp cloth and cut into chunks

50-100g granulated sugar

TOPPING:

300g plain flour

150g block margarine (cut into small pieces)

100g caster sugar

50g coconut } optional
25g porridge oats }

METHOD

1. Pre-heat oven to 160°C/350°F/Gas 5

2. Put the flour in a bowl. Rub in the margarine using your fingertips until the mixture resembles breadcrumbs. Stir in the coconut and porridge oats.

3. Stir in 100g caster sugar.

4. Put the chunks of rhubarb in 150ml water and granulated sugar in a saucepan. Stew gently until the rhubarb is just soft. Place in an ovenproof dish.

5. Spread topping over the stewed rhubarb.

6. Bake until the crumble is a pale gold colour. (Approx. 20-25 minutes)

SERVE

hot or cold with custard, ice cream or yoghurt.

Coconut and porridge oats are optional but add dietary fibre to the recipe.

Orange Cheesecake

(Serves 4-6)

INGREDIENTS

200g digestive biscuits
100g margarine
100g Philadelphia 'Light' Cheese.
$^1/_2$ orange jelly
1 small tin evaporated milk (170g)
25g caster sugar
Mandarin juice
Mandarin oranges

METHOD

1. Place digestive biscuits in a small plastic bag and crush with a rolling pin.

2. Melt the margarine in a small saucepan and stir the crushed biscuits into this, press the biscuit mix into a 22cm greased flan dish and leave to set.

3. Whisk evaporated milk until thick and creamy.

4. Beat the Philadelphia cheese and sugar together and add to evaporated milk.

5. Melt the jelly in 60ml mandarin juice in the microwave.

6. Slowly beat the jelly into the whisked mixture.

7. Pour this topping over the biscuit base and leave to set.

Decorate with sliced kiwi or mandarin oranges and cream rosettes if desired. To make cream rosettes put whipped cream into a piping bag fitted with a star nozzle and pipe out cream stars.

Charlotte Russe

(Serves 6)

INGREDIENTS
1 orange jelly
300ml boiling water
1-2 packets sponge finger
biscuits

FILLING:
2 separated eggs
150ml milk
60g caster sugar
15ml powdered gelatine
2-3 x 15ml water
150ml whipping cream
4 x 15ml sherry or whiskey

Purple or orange bow to
decorate.

METHOD
1. Line the bottom of 12.5cm Charlotte mould with a thin layer of jelly (3mm). Leave the rest of the Jelly to set.

2. When the jelly in the mould is set, decorate the sides of the mould with the sponge finger biscuits dipped in melted jelly to soften. N.B. the biscuits will need to be tapered so that they fit closely together. Place the sugary side next to the side of the mould.

3. Make custard with the 2 egg yolks, sugar and milk.

4. Dissolve the gelatine in the water and add to the custard when it has cooled.

5. Add the sherry. Leave aside.

6. When mixture shows signs of setting fold in stiffly beaten egg whites and lightly whipped cream.

7. Pour into the prepared mould and put aside to set.

TO SERVE:
8. Dip the mould into hot water

9. Invert onto a glass dish or compote.

10. Decorate with the remainder of the jelly, which has been finely chopped.

11. Tie a ribbon round the Charlotte Russe to complete.

Chocolate Mandarin Cheesecake

BASE
> 1 chocolate Swiss roll (380g)

TOPPING
> 1 (312g) can mandarin oranges
> 1 envelope gelatine
> 200g cottage cheese
> 300g cream cheese
> 100g caster sugar
> 1 x 5ml vanilla essence
> Cocoa powder for decoration

TO MAKE BASE:
1. Cut Swiss roll into 12 slices; cut each slice in half.

2. Arrange 10 half slices against inside of a deep, round 22cm, **loose-based** cake tin, rounded sides upwards.

3. Line base of tin with remaining Swiss roll.

4. Drain can of mandarin oranges and reserve the syrup in a small pyrex bowl.

5. Reserve 17 orange segments for decoration.

6. Use remaining orange segments up by placing one segment between each Swiss roll slice around the side of tin and then spread remaining segments evenly over the base.
See pic on page 47.

7. Sprinkle 2 x 15ml of reserved syrup on swiss roll base.

TO MAKE FILLING:
1. Sprinkle gelatine over remaining syrup in pyrex bowl.

2. Place bowl in a small saucepan of water over a moderate heat and stir gently until gelatine has dissolved.

3. Sieve cottage cheese into a mixing bowl.

4. Add cream cheese, caster sugar and vanilla essence.

5. Mix together using an electric beater (handheld).

6. Add dissolved gelatine and beat until smooth.

7. Pour cheese mixture over base in tin and level top with the back of a metal spoon.

8. Leave in the fridge for 1hr to set.

TO SERVE:

1. Remove cheesecake from tin by placing on a large lidded jar and gently pulling down the sides of the cake tin away from the base.

2. Cheesecake may be left on cake tin base and placed on a plate or eased off base with a palette knife and place on a serving plate.

3. Sieve a little cocoa powder over the cheesecake.

4. Arrange reserved orange segments around top edge of cheesecake to decorate.

5. Keep refrigerated until ready to serve.

May the saddest day of your future
Be no worse than the happiest day of your past.

Sponge Flan

(Serves 4-5)

INGREDIENTS

2 large eggs
50g caster sugar
50g plain flour
5ml caster sugar ⎤ **combined**
5ml plain flower ⎦ **for dusting**

METHOD

1. Prepare flan tin, grease well and line centre, dust the tin with a mixture of flour and caster sugar.

2. Whisk eggs and sugar until **thick** and creamy.

3. Gently fold in sieved flour with a metal tablespoon.

4. Bake in centre of oven for 20-30 minutes at 160°C/350°F/Gas 5.

5. Carefully turn onto a cooling tray.

SPONGE FRUIT FLAN

FILLING:

Tin of peaches - Strain off liquid and arrange fruit in flan case.

Quick Gel - make Quick Gel following instructions on packet but use 100ml of water (or fruit juice and water) and pour over arranged fruit.

This recipe is used as the basis for the next two recipes.

Hawaiian Pineapple Flan

(Serves 4-5)

INGREDIENTS

1 sponge flan (see p.49)
1 large can pineapple rings
75g soft margarine
75g light soft brown sugar
50g desiccated coconut
3 x 15ml milk
4 glacé cherries
5 diamonds of angelica } **Optional**

METHOD

1. Stand the flan case on the rack of the grill pan.

2. Pour a little of the juice from the can of pineapple rings over the sponge.

3. Arrange the pineapple rings, slightly overlapping, around the flan case with one ring in the centre.

4. Cream the margarine with the sugar and when it is soft and fluffy mix in the coconut and milk.

5. Spread this over the pineapple.

6. Cut 3 cherries in half and arrange them around the edge with a whole cherry in the centre, surrounded with angelica diamonds.

7. Put the flan case under a pre-heated grill.

8. Cook it until the topping is golden brown.

9. Serve the flan hot or cold with cream.

Baked Alaska

(Serves 4-5)

INGREDIENTS

1 sponge flan (see p.49)
1 large can sliced peaches
1 family block of vanilla ice cream
2 large egg whites
100g caster sugar

METHOD

1. Pre-heat oven to 190°C/450°F/Gas8.

2. Place flan case on an ovenproof plate.

3. Pour a little of the peach juice over the sponge flan. Arrange peach slices in the flan, and leave in a cool place.

4. Whisk the egg whites until they are stiff.

5. Whisk in half the sugar and continue whisking until the original stiffness is regained.

6. Fold in remaining sugar.

7. Lay the ice cream on top of the peaches, then carefully spread over the meringue to completely encase and seal the filling.

8. Bake the dessert on the centre shelf of a hot oven until golden brown, 3-5 mins.

9. Serve immediately.

Mince Pies

(makes 20-24 mince pies)

INGREDIENTS

FOR THE SHORTCRUST PASTRY:
225g plain flour, 125g butter, Pinch of salt, 10ml icing sugar. A little beaten egg to bind (and 1 egg beaten with a pinch of salt and use to glaze)

FOR THE FILLING:

Make and leave to "Mature" for 2 wks before using.
2 cooking apples, 2 lemons, 450g beef suet or butter, Pinch of salt, 110g mixed peel, 2 tablespoons orange marmalade, 225g currants, 225g sultanas, 900g Barbados sugar, 65ml Whiskey

METHOD

1. Core and bake the apples in a moderate oven 160°C/350°F/Gas Mark 4-5 for about 45 minutes. Allow to cool. When they are soft, remove the skin and mash the flesh into a pulp.

2. Grate the rind from the lemons on the finest part of a stainless steel grater and squeeze out the juice.

3. Add the other ingredients one by one, and as they are added, mix everything thoroughly.

4. Put into jars, cover with jam covers and leave to mature for 2 weeks before using.

5. Pre-heat the oven to 160°C/350°F/Gas 4-5. Keeping pastry ingredients as cool as possible, sieve the flour into a large bowl with the salt.

6. Cut the butter into cubes and rub into the flour using your fingertips. When the mixture looks like coarse breadcrumbs, stop.

7. Whisk the egg using a fork, add just enough beaten egg, or egg yolk and water, to bring the pastry together, then collect it into a ball with your hands, and decide whether you need a few more drops of liquid, although rather damp pastry is easier to handle and roll out, the resulting crust can be tough, drier pastry will give a crispier, 'shorter' crust.

8. Cover with clingfilm and leave to "rest" for 1 hour in the fridge (helps prevent shrinkage).

9. Roll out the pastry until quite thin, cut out using a 7.5cm diameter pastry cutter and line greased shallow bun tins.

10. Put a good teaspoon of mincemeat into each base, damp the edges with water and put another pastry circle on top. Use any scraps of pastry to make leaves, holly berries etc. for top of pies. Brush with beaten egg.

11. Bake the pies for 20 minutes. Allow them to cool slightly, and then dredge with icing sugar.

Chocolate Mousse

(Serves 4-5)

INGREDIENTS

410g tin evaporated milk
15ml cocoa powder
10ml coffee essence
60g caster sugar
A few drops of vanilla essence
1 sachet gelatine
45ml water
125ml whipping cream for decoration
50g grated chocolate for decoration

METHOD

1. Whisk evaporated milk until thick and creamy.

2. Dissolve gelatine following instructions on the packet.

3. Add cocoa powder, coffee essence, sugar and vanilla to whisked milk and mix well.

4. Slowly add gelatine to mixture.

5. Pour into individual glass dishes.

6. Decorate with grated chocolate and piped cream.

Raspberry Brulee

(Serves 4-5)

INGREDIENTS

150g raspberries
25g caster sugar
125ml raspberry yoghurt
200ml extra thick double cream
4 x 15ml demerara sugar

METHOD

1. Place 1 x 15ml of raspberries in the bottom of a ramekin dish.

2. Sprinkle with a little sugar.

3. Divide the yoghurt between the ramekins.

4. Divide the extra thick double cream between the ramekins.

5. Top each ramekin with 1 x 15ml Demerara sugar.

6. Grill quickly to caramelise, forming crunchy layer on top or use a cookery blowtorch, (this only takes a minute or two).

7. Serve immediately.

Cherry Cheesecake

(Serves 4-6)

INGREDIENTS

BASE:

200g digestive biscuits
100g polyunsaturated
margarine - melted

METHOD

1. Crush biscuits.

2. Put in a bowl add melted margarine. Press into greased flan tin (22cm).

3. Leave in fridge to harden (2hrs approx.).

FILLING:

1 x 36g pack Dream Topping
2.5ml vanilla essence
100g low fat soft cheese
125ml semi-skimmed milk
50g icing sugar
Juice of 1 lemon (small)
410g tin of red cherry pie filling

METHOD

1. Whip dream topping and milk, add sugar, vanilla essence and juice of lemon.

2. Add softened cheese. Beat well.

3. Pour on top of biscuit case and decorate with red cherry pie filling.

Orange Pavlova

INGREDIENTS
4 white eggs
200g caster sugar
4 x 5ml cornflour
2 x 5ml vinegar
2 x 2.5ml vanilla essence

FILLING:
6 x 15ml orange curd
2 x 15ml orange juice
125ml milk
2 egg yolks
15ml cornflour
125ml double cream
Tin of mandarin oranges
(drained)

METHOD
1. Place a sheet of non-stick baking paper on a baking tray.

2. Use a pencil to draw a 20cm circle using a saucepan lid as a guide.

3. Turn the paper over so the pencil mark does not come into contact with meringue.

4. Pre-heat oven to 130°C/275°F/Gas 1.

5. Whisk egg whites until stiff.

6. Whisk in half the sugar gradually.

7. Gradually fold in the remaining sugar with the cornflour, vinegar and vanilla essence.

8. Pile on to non-stick paper inside the circle.

9. Bake for about 1¼ hrs.

10. When cool invert onto a plate.

FILLING
1. Beat together the orange curd, orange juice, milk, egg yolks and cornflour in a saucepan over a gentle heat.

2. When thick allow to cool.

3. Whip the cream, pipe around the outer edge of the pavlova.

4. Spoon orange topping into the centre of the piped cream.

5. Arrange mandarin oranges over the filling.

6. Chill before serving.

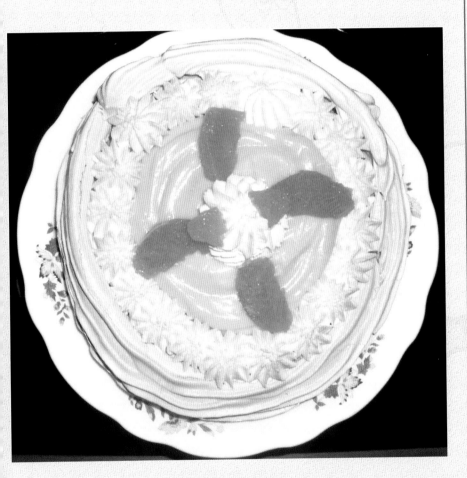

Orange Pavlova

Banoffi Pie

(Serves 6-8)

INGREDIENTS

12 digestive biscuits
100g margarine
1 tin condensed milk (397g)
2 large bananas
125ml whipping cream
1 chocolate flake

METHOD

1. Place the tin of condensed milk in a saucepan of boiling water (be careful) and simmer* gently for 2 hours. Make sure that there is plenty of water in the saucepan at all times.

2. While the tin of condensed milk is simmering, melt the butter in a saucepan over a low heat.

3. Place the biscuits in a plastic bag and crush using a wooden spoon.

4. Stir the biscuits into the melted butter. Spoon the mixture into the flan dish, covering the bottom evenly. Place in the fridge to set.

5. Just before you open the tin of condensed milk, chop the bananas into chunky rounds. Whip the cream until peaks begin to form on the surface.

6. Remove the tin of condensed milk from the water and run it under cold water to cool it. **Carefully** open the tin. At this stage the milk will have turned into a rich toffee mixture - be careful, the toffee mixture will be very hot.

7. Cover the biscuit base with the sliced bananas.

8. Pour the toffee over the biscuit base and spread with a knife (if the toffee is too thick to pour, spoon it out).

9. Spoon the cream over the toffee layer and sprinkle the chocolate flake over the top.

*To simmer - cook gently at just below boiling point.

Chrisтmas Pudding

(makes 2 x 850ml puddings)

INGREDIENTS

150g demerara sugar
150g suet
150g flour
150g fresh breadcrumbs
5 eggs
250g raisins
350g sultanas
Pinch of salt
Medium grated carrot
7.5ml mixed spice
7.5ml nutmeg
7.5ml cinnamon
5ml ground cloves
5ml treacle
5ml syrup
1/2 miniature Brandy/Whiskey
200g Glacé cherries
Large skinned apple - grated
or chopped
Juice of 1 lemon
Juice of 1 orange
Grated rind of 1 lemon

METHOD

1. Mix all the dry ingredients together.

2. Beat the eggs, Brandy, treacle, syrup, orange juice and lemon juice together.

3. Mix into the dry ingredients and stir well.

4. Fill 2 well-greased 850ml (1 1/2 lb) pudding basins, cover each basin with greased and pleated greaseproof paper, tie down tightly and steam for 6 hours.

5. Remove greaseproof paper and cover with lids, store in a cool, dry place until needed.

6. Steam again for another 4 hours when serving.

7. Serve with Brandy Butter.

BRANDY BUTTER

INGREDIENTS

50g butter
Brandy
50g Icing sugar

METHOD

Beat the sugar into the butter, gradually add the Brandy until the mixture resembles thick cream, serve in a sauceboat.

Cakes and Tray Bakes

May your glass be ever full.

Yoghurt Cake

INGREDIENTS

1 tub yoghurt (any flavour)
3 tubs self-raising flour.
1 ¹/₂ tubs caster sugar
1 tub cooking oil
3 medium eggs

METHOD

1. Empty the contents of the tub of yoghurt into a mixing bowl.

2. Wash out the yoghurt tub and use to measure the other ingredients.

3. Place all the ingredients in the mixing bowl, beat well, until smooth and well mixed.

4. Divide between 2 x 1lb greased and lined loaf tins.

5. Bake in a pre-heated oven at 160°C/350°F/Gas 5 for 45 minutes approx.

The cake shown is a peach yoghurt cake. This is achieved by using peach yoghurt and adding cut up sliced peaches to the mixture.

Tipsy Light Fruit Cake

INGREDIENTS
150g soft margarine
150g caster sugar
200g plain flour
3 large eggs
1 x 5ml baking powder
2 x 15ml milk
250g sultanas - soak overnight in 2 x 15ml whiskey

METHOD
1. Oven temp. 150°C/325°F/Gas 3. Prepare tin - grease and line sides and base.

2. Cream the margarine and sugar until soft and fluffy.

3. Gradually add the beaten eggs to the creamed mixture. (If mixture shows signs of curdling, fold in a little sieved flour).

4. Carefully fold in sieved flour followed by the sultanas.

5. Add the milk.

6. Place in prepared tin and bake for 1hr in a pre-heated oven then turn down oven to gas 2 for the last ¹/₂ hr, cover with tin foil to prevent over browning. Allow to cool in tin before turning on to a cooling tray.

7. When completely cold, store in an airtight tin.

Tip soaking the sultanas overnight in the whiskey helps to make this a lovely moist cake.

Valentine Cake

INGREDIENTS
150g soft margarine
150g caster sugar
150g self-raising flour
3 medium eggs
1 x 15ml strained lemon juice
1 x 15ml desiccated coconut

METHOD
1. Pre-heat oven,
   160°C/350°F/Gas 5.

2. Grease a heart shaped tin
   and line with greaseproof
   paper.

3. Cream margarine and
   sugar.

4. Gradually beat in the
   eggs.

5. Sieve and fold in the
   flour.

6. Fold in the lemon juice
   and coconut.

7. Place mixture in prepared
   tin and spread evenly.

8. Bake in centre of oven
   for 1 hour approx. or
   until golden and firm.

9. Cool in tin for a few
   minutes then turn on to a
   cooling tray.

BUTTER CREAM FOR CENTRE:
75g soft margarine or butter
150g icing sugar - sieve
1 x 15ml warm water

1. Cream the margarine (or
   butter) and icing sugar,
   beat in the water.

2. Cut the cake in to two,
   through the middle and
   use the butter cream to
   sandwich the two halves
   together.

*"Ready to roll icing" can be used to
decorate the top of the cake.*

Lemon Cake

INGREDIENTS

LEMON CAKE:
110g soft margarine
175g caster sugar
175g self-raising flour
4 x 15ml milk
Grated zest of lemon
2 medium eggs
Pinch of salt

LEMON SYRUP:
4 x 15ml fresh lemon juice (1 large lemon), 75g icing sugar

TO FINISH:
Icing sugar

METHOD
1. Grease 2lb loaf tin and line with greaseproof paper (or line with a loaf tin liner).
2. Pre-heat oven 160°C/350°F/Gas 5.
3. Place all ingredients in a bowl and mix for 3 minutes.
4. Put in mixture in prepared loaf tin. Bake for 45-55 mins until firm to touch well risen and golden brown.
5. Leave in tin to cool on a cooling tray.
6. Gently warm lemon and icing sugar in a pan until sugar dissolves.
7. Prick cake all over with a fork. Pour warmed lemon syrup over the top.
8. Leave until cake is cold before turning out.
9. Serve sprinkled with icing sugar.

Fifteens

INGREDIENTS

Fifteen digestive biscuits
218g tin condensed milk (small tin)
15 glace cherries
15 marshmallows
Desiccated coconut

METHOD

1. Place digestive biscuits in a freezer bag, tie end closed and crush with a rolling pin. Alternatively, use a small blender.

2. Cut marshmallows and cherries to desired size using scissors. (Have a glass of hot water handy to clean scissors as this allows for easier cutting of the marshmallows).

3. Place cherries, marshmallows and condensed milk into a large bowl and mix well.

4. Liberally sprinkle some coconut on to a large piece of tin foil. Place the mixture on top of this and roll out, sprinkling more coconut on top and on the sides.

5. When rolled into the desired length and thickness (long sausage shape), wrap tinfoil around it and place in fridge for a few hours to harden.

6. Cut into slices and enjoy!!

N.B. could be rolled into individual balls. Also, doubling the ingredients results in using a large tin of condensed milk, 1 packet of marshmallows, large packet of digestive biscuits and nearly a small container of cherries.

Caramel Squares

INGREDIENTS
BASE:
150g plain flour
100g soft margarine
50g caster sugar

CARAMEL:
100g margarine
100g caster sugar or brown sugar (dark or light)
1 dessertspoon syrup
1 small tin condensed milk
Vanilla essence

TOP:
12 squares cooking chocolate

METHOD
1. Pre-heat oven 160°C/350°F/Gas 5.
2. Cream margarine and sugar.
3. Add flour.
4. Press into a small greased Swiss roll tin (28cm x 18cm).
5. Bake for 20 - 25 minutes until golden. Cool.
6. Place caramel ingredients in a small saucepan, heat slowly stirring continuously until mixture melts and boils (mixture will become thicker and darker in colour). DO NOT ALLOW TO BURN!
7. Pour over cooked base, leave to set.
8. Place chocolate in a small bowl, place this over a saucepan of boiling water - leave to melt.
9. Spread over caramel - leave to set, cut into squares.

Queen Cakes

(makes 12)

INGREDIENTS
100g soft margarine
100g caster sugar
2 eggs
100g plain flour
1 x 5ml baking powder
50g dried fruit

METHOD

1. Pre-heat the oven 180°C/425°F/Gas 7.

2. Place 12 paper bun cases in a bun tray.

7. Sieve the flour and baking powder onto a plate.

8. Beat the margarine, caster sugar and eggs together in a bowl with a wooden spoon or electric whisk.

9. Fold in the flour and baking powder with a large metal spoon.

10. Add the dried fruit.

11. Divide the mixture evenly between the paper cases.

12. Place the tray on the upper shelf of the oven.

13. Bake for 10 - 15 minutes until risen and golden brown.

14. Cool on a wire rack. Store in an airtight tin.

Orange Princess Biscuits

INGREDIENTS

200g soft margarine
50g icing sugar
Rind of 1 large orange
200g plain flour

DECORATION

100g cooking chocolate

METHOD

1. Cream margarine and sieved icing sugar together until very soft.

2. Add grated orange rind and gradually work in the flour.

3. Put the mixture into a forcing bag fitted with a large star pipe and pipe into finger shapes.

4. Leave in a fridge for 15 mins.

5. Bake in a moderately heated oven for approximately 15-20 mins at 160°C/350°F/Gas 5.

6. Cool biscuits before dipping the ends in the melted chocolate.

N.B. Slant piping bag to keep fingers thin. Don't make them too long.

Meringues

INGREDIENTS
3 white eggs
150g caster sugar

METHOD
1. Whisk the egg whites until very stiff.

2. Beat in half the caster sugar, a little at a time, beat well between each addition.

3. Fold in the remaining sugar.

4. Pipe meringues in rosettes on to Bakewell non-stick paper covering a baking sheet.

5. Put the meringues in a very cool oven on the bottom shelf - 100°C/200°F/Gas¼ for 2 hours to dry.

6. Store in an airtight tin. Will keep up to 3 weeks.

TIP: These meringues also freeze well.

Flakemeal Biscuits

(makes 30 approx.)

INGREDIENTS

200g margarine
100g caster sugar
250g flakemeal
5ml salt
Pinch of baking soda
50g coconut
100g plain flour

METHOD

1. Pre-heat oven 160°C/350°F/Gas 5.

2. Cream the butter and sugar together and gradually work in the other ingredients.

3. Turn on to a surface sprinkled with flakemeal and roll out.

4. Score attractively with a fork and cut into biscuits

5. Bake for approx. 20 mins. Until golden brown.

TIP: These biscuits can be dusted with caster sugar when removed from the oven, or left to cool slightly before dipping one side in melted chocolate. For this amount of biscuits, approximately 75g of chocolate should be enough.

LEFT: Flakemeal Biscuits
MIDDLE: Meringues
RIGHT: Orange Princess Biscuits

Coconut Biscuits

(makes 24)

INGREDIENTS

100g soft margarine
$1/2$ beaten egg
100g coconut
100g caster sugar
150g self-raising flour
1 x 5ml vanilla essence
A few chopped cherries

METHOD

1. Pre-heat the oven to 160°C/350°F/Gas 5.

2. Cream the margarine and sugar.

3. Add the beaten egg and vanilla essence.

4. Gradually add the sieved flour.

5. Gradually add the coconut.

6. Divide the mixture in half, then quarters and then eights. Divide each portion into three (24 pieces) and roll into a ball shape.

7. Place each ball on a greased baking sheet and flatten slightly.

8. Place a piece of cherry in the centre of each and bake for approximately 15 minutes until a very pale golden colour.

9. Remove and allow to cool on a wire rack.

Easter Chocolate Nests

INGREDIENTS

50g Rice Krispies
100g (8 squares) cooking chocolate
Smartie eggs

METHOD

1. Break up the chocolate and put in a Pyrex bowl.

2. Melt the chocolate by placing the Pyrex bowl over a saucepan of water and heat gently until the chocolate melts. It is important that the water does not get into the chocolate, so the bowl must be bigger than the saucepan.

3. When the chocolate is melted CAREFULLY remove the bowl from the saucepan.

4. Mix in the Rice Krispies until they are well coated.

5. Place a spoonful into each section of a bun tray. Form into the shape of a nest using a teaspoon.

6. Place a few Smartie eggs in each nest.

Easter Simnel Cake

A tasty rich fruitcake with a layer of marzipan cooked in the centre of the cake and after baking finish with a decorative layer of marzipan on the top.

INGREDIENTS
FOR ALMOND PASTE
150g ground almonds
75g caster sugar
75g sieved icing sugar
Almond essence (a few drops)
Beaten egg to mix

METHOD
1. Mix all the dry ingredients together, flavour with the almond essence.

2. Mix to a stiff paste with the egg.

3. Roll this out to the exact dimensions of the cake tin (in this case a 20cm diameter tin is used). The marzipan needs to fit inside the tin.

THE CAKE MIXTURE:
150g butter
150g caster sugar
4 eggs
150g plain flour
2.5ml baking powder
2 x 5ml mixed spice
200g sultanas

200g raisins
50g cherries
20cm diameter cake tin
(approx 10cm deep)

METHOD
1. Prepare the cake tin by lining the sides and bottom with greaseproof paper. Grease the paper. Pre-heat the oven. Oven temperature: 150°C/325°F/Gas 3.

2. Cream the butter and sugar.

3. Add the beaten eggs gradually.

4. Fold in the flour and baking powder plus the mixed spice.

5. Stir in the fruit.

6. Put half the mixture into the cake, lay the almond paste on top, press gently into position and cover with the remaining cake mixture.

7. Bake in the pre-heated oven for about 2½ hours.

8. When cooked allow to cool in the tin, then remove from the tin, peel off the lining paper and wrap in tinfoil.

9. Store until you are ready to decorate the cake.

ALMOND PASTE FOR DECORATING:
200g ground almonds
100g caster sugar
100g sieved icing sugar
Almond essence (a few drops)
Beaten egg to mix and for attaching almond paste
apricot jam.

METHOD
1. Make as before and keep about one third to use for the decorations.

2. Roll two thirds to the size of the top of the cake.

3. Brush the top of the cake with a little jam and turn on to the prepared almond paste.

4. Press well together and neaten the edges with a knife.

5. Turn right side up and decorate.

DECORATIONS
1. Press the almond paste with a wire cake cooler, this gives a decoration of neat little squares.

2. Then pinch round the edges and decorate the top with balls of marzipan, stuck in position with beaten egg. These are usually placed to form a circle round the edge of the cake.

3. Brush the balls with more egg and brown under a moderate grill. Leave like this or ice the layer of almond paste with a layer of royal icing combining the modern and traditional and decorate with small Easter eggs and fluffy chickens. A very simple decoration can be made from broken half eggshells, which have been **washed** and dried and then painted prettily and arranged on top of the cake with an Easter chicken set in the middle. A cleaned egg shell could be painted on the inside with melted chocolate.

4. Set on a cake board and put an Easter frill round the cake.

Marry a woman out of the glens and you marry the whole glen.
Pós bean as glean is pós faidh tú an glean uilig.

Mars Bar Krispies

INGREDIENTS

100g block margarine
100g Rice Krispies
4 large Mars bars
200g cooking chocolate

METHOD

1. Melt the margarine and the Mars bars very slowly in a Pyrex bowl over a saucepan of steaming water.

2. Add the Rice Krispies and mix until they are well coated.

3. Spoon into a greased Swiss roll tin (27cm x 18cm) and spread evenly.

4. Melt the chocolate again in a bowl over a saucepan of steaming water and spread over the mixture, sprinkle with sugar strands.

5. When set cut into squares.

Butterfly Buns

INGREDIENTS
100g soft margarine
100g caster sugar
2 eggs
125g self-raising flour

DECORATION:
40g soft margarine
80g icing sugar (sieve)
Approx. 1 x 15ml milk
Little extra icing sugar for dusting

METHOD
1. Pre-heat oven to 160°C/350°F/Gas 5.
2. Place 12 bun cases in a bun tray.
3. Lightly beat the 2 eggs.
4. Sieve the flour.
5. Beat together the margarine and sugar until smooth and creamy.
6. Gradually add the beaten eggs.
7. Fold in the flour.
8. Divide the mixture evenly between the paper cases.
9. Bake for 15 - 20 minutes until risen and golden brown.
10. Remove from oven and place on a cooling tray and allow to cool.
11. Prepare the butter icing by beating the margarine, icing sugar and milk together until light and fluffy.
12. Assemble the butterfly buns (**as on next page**) and dust with the extra icing sugar.

Making the Butterfly Buns

1. Cut off the top of each cake.

2. Cut this in half.

3. Fill the centre with butter-cream and position wings in place.

Marshmallow Cushions

INGREDIENTS
50g block margarine
2 x 15ml golden syrup
200g milk cooking chocolate
200g Rich Tea Biscuits
100g raisins
200g marshmallows
PLUS: 15 squares milk cooking chocolate to cover

METHOD
1. Use the microwave on full power for 1 minute approx. to melt margarine, syrup and chocolate (200g chocolate).

2. Use a food processor to chop up the biscuits and marshmallows.

3. Add the chopped biscuits and marshmallows to the melted mixture along with the raisins.

4. Once the mixture has been well mixed. Place in an oblong greased Swiss roll tin (28cm x 18cm). Allow to harden.

5. Break cooking chocolate into small pieces place in a small pyrex bowl or a plastic bowl, microwave on medium 50% power for 1$^{1}/_{2}$ mins, stir well, heat in further bursts of 30 seconds on medium until melted. Stir well to ensure fully melted. For different microwaves adjust accordingly.

6. Pour melted chocolate over marshmallow and biscuit base. Smooth with a knife. Leave to set.

7. When the chocolate is set cut into squares. Store in airtight tin.

Mini Chocolate Muffins

(makes 24)

INGREDIENTS

150g plain flour
2 x 15ml cocoa powder
1 x 10ml baking powder
1 x 1.25ml salt
1 medium egg lightly beaten
50g golden caster sugar
50g margarine melted and
cooled slightly
50g grated cooking chocolate
150ml milk

DECORATIONS:

Melted milk chocolate
Melted white chocolate
White chocolate buttons
Milk chocolate buttons
Smarties

METHOD

1. Turn on oven to 170°C/400°F/Gas 6.

2. Sieve the flour, cocoa powder, baking powder and salt into a large bowl.

3. Mix the egg, sugar, milk and cooled melted margarine in another bowl.

4. Add the wet ingredients (all of No 3) to the dry ingredients (all of No 2).

5. Mix together quickly. Mixture should look lumpy. Add the grated chocolate and stir in.

6. Divide the mixture between the muffin cases. One 5ml spoon in each.

7. Bake towards the top of the oven for 10 minutes.

8. Allow to cool for 5 minutes in the tins before transferring them to a cooling tray.

9. When cold, dip into either milk or white melted chocolate and top with a button of the opposite colour or a smartie.

10. When chocolate has set, dust with icing sugar if desired.

Chocolate Muffins

(makes 12)

INGREDIENTS

1 x 15ml cocoa powder
200g plain flour
2 x 5ml baking powder
175g caster sugar
A pinch of salt
100g melted block margarine (cooled)
2 medium eggs
200ml milk approx.
2.5ml vanilla essence
100g chocolate chips

METHOD

1. Pre-heat oven to 160°C/350°F/Gas 5

2. Sieve the cocoa powder, flour, baking powder and salt into a large bowl.

3. Add the caster sugar, chocolate chips and mix well.

4. Beat the eggs and milk together and add the vanilla essence.

5. Make a well in the centre of the dry ingredients and pour in the melted margarine, milk and egg mixture and vanilla.

6. Spoon into 12 muffin cases and bake for 15 - 20 minutes.

7. Cool on a wire tray before storing in an airtight tin.

Double Chocolate Chip Muffins

(makes 20)

INGREDIENTS

8 x 15ml cocoa powder
450g plain flour
2 x 15ml baking powder
5ml bicarbonate of sugar
4 x 15ml caster sugar
6 x 15ml brown sugar
2 eggs
500ml of milk
Pinch of salt
100g melted margarine
(cooled)
200g dark chocolate grated
200g white chocolate grated

METHOD

1. Pre-heat oven to 170°C/400°F/Gas 6.

2. Place 20 large, paper muffin cases in deep muffin tins.

3. Sieve all the dry ingredients into a bowl, and make a well in the centre.

4. Beat egg, milk and salt and add to dry ingredients with the melted, cooled margarine.

5. Lightly beat mixture until combined but still slightly lumpy. Don't over beat.

6. Gently fold in grated dark chocolate and grated milk chocolate.

7. Three quarters fill the muffin cases with the mixture.

8. Bake for about 20 minutes or until an inserted skewer comes out clean.

9. Cool on a wire tray.

STORAGE: Once cold, you can keep muffins in an airtight container for up to 2 days.

Chocolate Slab Cake (All in One Method)

(makes 24)

INGREDIENTS
150g soft margarine
150g caster sugar
150g self-raising flour
5ml baking powder
3 small eggs
15ml cocoa powder (sieve)
15ml milk

METHOD
1. Pre-heat oven 160°C/350°F/Gas 5. Place all the above ingredients in a mixing bowl. Using a hand held electric beater mix for 4-5 minutes.

2. Put into prepared cake tin (26cm x 16.5cm x 3cm), lined and greased and bake for 25 - 30 mins. When well risen and firm to touch, remove from oven. Turn onto cooling tray and leave to cool.

TOPPING:
50g soft margarine
100g icing sugar

DECORATIONS
1. Cream margarine and sugar until soft and fluffy.

2. Spread over cold slab cake and decorate as required (e.g. crushed chocolate flake, chocolate vermicelli or chocolate buttons).

Malteser Biscuits

INGREDIENTS

13 Digestive Biscuits, crushed
100g butter/margarine
175g cooking chocolate
1 x 5ml vanilla essence
200g Maltesers
2 x 5ml golden syrup
200g white chocolate

METHOD

1. Melt butter and cooking chocolate, gently in a pyrex bowl over a saucepan of warm water. Add vanilla essence and syrup.

2. Remove from heat and add whole Maltesers and crushed biscuits.

3. Press into a small greased Swiss roll tin (28cm x 18cm) and spread evenly.

4. Decorate with melted white chocolate or additional cooking chocolate with white chocolate swirled through it. Leave to set and cut into squares.

Shortbread

(makes 45-50 pieces approx.)

INGREDIENTS

400g butter
200g caster sugar
400g plain flour
50g cornflour
50g rice flour
Pinch of salt
Yolk of 1 egg

METHOD

1. Pre-heat oven to 150°C/325°F/Gas 3.

2. Sieve flour, cornflour, salt and rice flour together.

3. Beat butter and sugar (not too soft).

4. Add half the flour mixture.

5. Add egg yolk and mix.

6. Add remainder of the flour mixture.

7. Knead together into a lump.

8. Roll out on a table top dusted with cornflour and plain flour.

9. Cut out with round cutters (or depending on season, Christmas or Easter shapes).

10. Place on baking sheets not too close together.

11. Cook for 20 minutes approx. until pale gold.

12. Dust with caster sugar.

13. Store in an airtight tin, putting greaseproof paper between each layer of shortbread.

Banana Muffins

(makes 10)

INGREDIENTS
255g plain flour
15ml baking powder
2.5ml baking soda (bicarbonate of soda)
30 ml caster sugar
45ml light brown sugar
1 egg
250ml milk
Pinch of salt
50g margarine melted and cooled
2 large ripe bananas

METHOD
1. Pre-heat the oven to 170°C/400°F/Gas 6.

2. Place 10 large, paper muffin cases in deep muffin tins.

3. Sieve **all** the dry ingredients into a bowl and make a well in the centre.

4. Beat egg and milk together. Add to dry ingredients with the melted, cooled margarine.

5. Lightly beat mixture until combined but still slightly lumpy. Don't overbeat.

6. Mash the bananas well, and then fold into the mixture.

7. Three-quarters fill the muffin cases with the mixture.

8. Bake for about 20 minutes, or until an inserted skewer comes out clean.

9. Cool on a wire cooling tray.

10. When cold store in an airtight tin.

Christmas Cake

INGREDIENTS

200g butter
200g soft brown sugar
200g plain flour
100g ground almonds
800g mixed fruit
100g cherries
2.5ml mixed spice
2.5ml cinnamon
2.5ml ginger
2.5ml nutmeg
5 eggs
15ml gravy browning
30ml Whiskey/Brandy

METHOD

1. Prepare 23cm round tin, line with a double thickness of greaseproof paper, grease tin and paper.

2. Tie brown paper round the outside higher than edge of tin, with cord.

3. Cream butter and sugar until almost white.

4. Gradually add beaten eggs, add a little flour if necessary to prevent curdling.

5. Add the sieved flour, spices and ground almonds, then add the gravy browning.

6. Half the cherries and add along with the rest of the fruit.

7. Place in a tin, make a hollow in the centre.

8. Leave for a while. Heat oven for 10 minute before putting cake in at 150°C/325°F/Gas 3 and cook for 1 hour.

9. Then lower to 140°C/300°F/Gas 2 for 1 hour, and then 130°C/275°F/Gas 1 for 1 hour.

10. Test with skewer to see if cake is cooked. Push skewer into centre of cake, if skewer comes out without any cake mixture attached the cake is cooked.

11. Remove from oven.

12. Leave in tin overnight. Cover with greaseproof paper but first prick all over 2cm apart and pour brandy over cake.

13. The next day, wrap in greaseproof paper and tinfoil. Store in an airtight tin.

ALMOND PASTE
INGREDIENTS

300g ground almonds
150g caster sugar
150g sieved icing sugar
2 drops almond essence
1 large egg
1 x 10ml Brandy/Sherry
2.5ml vanilla essence

METHOD

1. Mix all the dry ingredients together, flavour with the almond essence, Brandy/Sherry and vanilla essence.

2. Mix to a stiff paste with the egg.

3. Divide into one third and two thirds. Use the one third to cover the top of the cake and the two thirds to do round the sides; pieces of string cut to size will be useful for measuring.

ROYAL ICING
INGREDIENTS

3 - 4 egg whites
600g - 800g sieved icing sugar
1 - 2 drops fresh lemon juice
1 - 2 drops glycerine

METHOD

1. Sieve icing sugar.

2. Place egg whites in a bowl and beat lightly with a fork until frothy.

3. Place icing sugar gradually, 15ml at a time, beating thoroughly between each addition until the mixture is smooth, shiny, white and the consistency of very stiff meringue.

4. It should be thin enough to spread and work with but thick enough to hold its shape when spread in peaks.

5. At this stage beat in glycerine and lemon juice.

6. Cover with a damp cloth and leave to stand for about an hour.

7. Run a palette knife across surface to burst bubbles, bang bowl lightly on table to bring up any more bubbles, and run palette knife across the surface again lightly.

8. Always keep the bowl covered with a damp cloth.

9. Place cake on a cake board on an up-turned mixing bowl.

10. Spread icing very thickly over cake, taking care to cover completely.

11. Lift icing up in peaks with sticky palette knife, all over cake to represent snow and decorate with suitable figures - trees, holly, Santa, and churches etc.

Bread and Scones

*May the roof over your head be always strong.
And may you be in Heaven half an hour
Before the Devil knows you're dead!*

Potato Bread

INGREDIENTS
200g mashed potatoes
15g plain flour
25g butter
1 x 5ml salt
Margarine needed for greasing griddle

METHOD
1. Wash, peel and boil potatoes until soft (20-30 mins) Drain and then mash until smooth.

2. Place in a bowl. Add flour, salt and butter.

3. Knead well together.

4. Divide into two, roll each $1/2$ into a circle and cut into quarters, prick with a fork.

5. Place on a greased griddle, brown on 1 side.

6. Turn and brown the other side.

7. Serve either hot or cold.

Potato Apple

INGREDIENTS
4 good pinches of salt
200g self-raising flour
4 large cooking apples
1kg potatoes
Some cooking oil

TO SERVE:
Butter
Sugar

METHOD

1. Wash, peel and boil the potatoes before mashing them.

2. When mashed sieve in the flour and salt.

3. Beat well.

4. Work the mixture lightly with your hand to make a pliable dough, adding a little more flour if it is needed.

5. Cut the dough in two and roll out the first piece using a well floured board and rolling pin.

6. Depending on the size required use a small or big sieve to cut out the size desired. Do the same with the other half of the dough.

7. Chop the apples until very fine and spread one of the potato rounds with plenty of apple.

8. Cover with another round and neaten the edges by pressing a fork all the way round the edges as for a piece of shortbread.

9. Cook gently on both sides in a heavy based oiled pan or on a greased griddle.

10. When well browned, open, sprinkle with sugar and add a generous slice of butter, close again and serve very hot.

Pancakes

INGREDIENTS
100g plain flour
Pinch of salt
2 eggs
250ml milk
Lard or oil for frying

METHOD
1. Sieve flour and salt into a bowl.
2. Make a well in the centre, add the eggs and a little of the milk.
3. Beat with a wooden spoon, gradually incorporating the flour.
4. As the mixture thickens gradually add half the milk.
5. Beat well until smooth.
6. Add remaining milk, and beat until bubbly on top.
7. Heat a little lard or oil in a frying pan, barely covering the base.
8. When a slight haze rises, pour in enough batter to cover base of pan thinly (2 x 15ml), tilting pan to make sure batter covers base evenly.
9. Cook for about 1 minute over a high heat until browned underneath.
10. Toss or turn pancake over, cook other side for about $^1/_2$ minute. Repeat until batter is used.
11. Place cooked pancake on a plate and keep warm in the oven.
12. Repeat process until all the batter has been used.

    (For sweet pancakes, add 5ml caster sugar to the batter).

SAUCE FOR PANCAKES:
75g butter
75g caster sugar
Finely grated rind of 1 lemon
$^1/_2$ orange, juice and finely grated rind
2 x 15ml Cointreau

Melt butter in a frying pan. Add sugar, lemon rind, orange rind and orange juice. Bring mixture to the boil. Add Cointreau and boil for a few minutes until syrupy. Fold pancakes in 4 and pour the syrup on top. Serve with a scoop of ice cream beside the pancake.

Pancakes can also be filled with cooked minced beef, onion and tomato puree to make savoury pancakes.

Waffles

INGREDIENTS

200g plain flour
50g caster sugar
15ml baking powder
2.5ml salt
2 eggs (beaten)
75g butter
350ml milk

METHOD

1. Place dry ingredients in a bowl and mix together.

2. Add in eggs, butter and half of the milk and beat until smooth.

3. Add remainder of milk and mix together.

(Alternatively place all ingredients in a food processor and process until smooth.)

To cook Waffles: Pre-heat a waffle maker. Put 3 x 15ml of mixture into the waffle maker, close and cook until golden brown. Serve hot with butter, maple syrup, cream cheese, sliced apples or crispy bacon.

Banana Bread

INGREDIENTS

75g soft margarine
100g caster sugar
1 medium egg
2 small ripe bananas
150g wholemeal flour
1 x 5ml baking powder
1 x 15ml warm water

METHOD

1. Pre-heat oven 160°C/350°F/Gas5.

2. Grease a 1lb loaf tin and line base (or use 1lb loaf tin liner - no further lining or greasing required).

3. Cream margarine and sugar until light and fluffy.

4. Beat in egg.

5. Mash bananas with a fork and beat into mixture.

6. Sieve flour and baking powder and beat into banana mixture.

7. Stir in water.

8. Put into prepared tin and bake 45-55 minutes.

9. Leave in tin to cool for 10 minutes. Then turn on to a wire tray.

May the road rise to meet you.
May the wind be always at your back.
May the sun shine warm upon your face;
The rains fall soft upon your fields.
And until we meet again,
May God hold you in the hollow of his hand.

Oven Wheaten

INGREDIENTS

300g wheaten bread ready mix
25g margarine
25g caster sugar
200 - 250ml buttermilk

METHOD

1. Pre-heat oven to 170°C/400°F/Gas 6.

2. Grease an 18cm diameter sandwich tin.

3. Rub margarine into the flour using your fingertips.

4. Stir in sugar.

5. Using a knife mix to elastic dough with buttermilk.

6. Turn on to a floured board. Knead lightly. Place in prepared sandwich tin.

7. Make into farls. Bake for 40 - 45 minute until well risen.

COOKERY TIP: The bread should sound hollow when lightly tapped on the base.

Fruit Loaf

INGREDIENTS

200g plain flour
25g margarine
25g caster sugar
4 - 5 glacé cherries chopped
50g sultanas
125mls buttermilk
1 x 5ml baking soda
1 x 5ml cream of tartar

METHOD

1. Pre-heat oven 170°C/400°F/Gas 6. Sieve flour, baking soda, and cream of tartar into a mixing bowl.
2. Rub in margarine.
3. Stir in sugar, sultanas and chopped cherries.
4. Mix to an elastic consistency with buttermilk.
5. Knead lightly.
6. Place in a lightly greased and floured loaf tin (1lb).
7. Bake for 25 -30 minutes approx.

Plain Scones

INGREDIENTS

240g soda bread flour
100g margarine
100g caster sugar
250ml Buttermilk Approx.
1 egg

METHOD

1. Pre-heat oven 180°C/425°F/Gas 7. Sieve flour.

2. Rub in margarine.

3. Add sugar.

4. Mix to a soft dough, yet firm enough to handle, with the buttermilk and egg.

5. Roll out on a lightly floured surface and cut into scones 1.5cm thick, using a 6cm cutter.

8. Place on a floured baking tray.

9. Bake in a hot oven for approx. 10-15 minutes.

Variations

SULTANA

Add 50g-75g of sultanas to rubbed in mixture.

ORANGE

Grated rind and juice of 1 orange, sugar cubes. Add rind to rubbed in mixture. When scones have been cut out, dip a lump of sugar into orange juice and immediatley press gently into the centre of a scone. Repeat process for each scone.

CHEESE & ONION

2ml mustard powder sieve with flour and salt.
80g margarine (instead of 100g)
$^{1}/_{2}$ small onion finely chopped

75-100g grated cheddar cheese
Add onion and grated cheese to rubbed in mixture.

> **TIP: Scones are best eaten on the day they are made.**

Drinks

He who drinks only water will not be drunk
An té ólas acht uisge ní bheidhi sé air

Irish Coffee

INGREDIENTS

35ml Irish Whiskey - as smooth as the wit of the land
6 white or brown sugar cubes - as sweet as the tongue of a rogue
Freshly made strong coffee - as strong as a friendly hand
Fresh Double Cream - as rich as an Irish brogue

METHOD

1. Heat a stemmed glass or whiskey goblet with hot water, not boiling, then discard the water.

2. Pour in the Irish Whiskey, then add the sugar cubes.

3. Add the fresh coffee to within an inch of the rim and stir to dissolve the sugar.

4. Top off to the brim with lightly whipped double cream so that the cream floats on top. Pour the cream slowly on to the coffee over the back of a spoon, this causes the cream to form a 'head' on the top of the coffee.

DO NOT STIR after adding the cream, as the true flavour is obtained by drinking the hot coffee and Irish Whiskey through the cream.

SLAINTE!!! (Good Health)

Health and long life to you.
Land without rent to you.
A child every year to you, and may you die in Ireland.

By permission of the "Old Bushmills Distillery"

Hot Toddy

INGREDIENTS

35ml Irish whiskey
7.5ml brown sugar
5 cloves
2 lemon slices

METHOD

1. Warm a stemmed glass/goblet with a little hot water not boiling, then discard the water.

2. Put brown sugar in the warmed glass. Add enough boiling water to dissolve the sugar. A metal spoon should be put in the glass to prevent the hot water shattering the glass.

3. Add the Whiskey, cloves and sliced lemon.

4. Top with more boiling water and enjoy!

This is a traditional Irish nightcap.
The word "whiskey" comes from the Irish
"uisce beatha" - water of life.

Banana Milkshake

(Serves 2)

INGREDIENTS
200ml semi-skimmed milk
2 bananas
2 - 3 scoops ice cream
4 ice cubes

TO DECORATE:
Chocolate flakes
Mini pink and white marshmallows

METHOD
1. Put all ingredients in a blender together and mix until smooth.

2. Pour into two glasses, decorate and serve.

Raspberry Delight

(Serves 1)

INGREDIENTS

2 handfuls raspberries

1 x 15ml orange curd

125ml double cream

1 scoop raspberry ripple ice cream

METHOD

1. Place all the ingredients in a blender and whisk until smooth.

2. Pour into a glass, decorate* and serve.

3. Indulge yourself!!!

* Suggestions for decorations -
orange rind, raspberry coulée
or mint leaves.

Four Fruit Smoothie

(Serves 4)

INGREDIENTS

1$^1/_2$ cups cranberry juice

6 medium/large sliced strawberries

1 small sliced banana

$^1/_2$ sliced mango

4 crushed ice cubes

METHOD

1. Place all the ingredients in a blender and whiz until smooth.

2. Pour into 4 glasses.

3. Indulge yourself!!!

Top tip! Crush the ice cubes by putting them in a bag, and then shatter them with a rolling pin.

Limeade

INGREDIENTS
3 limes
125g caster sugar
300ml boiling water
Pinch of salt
Ice cubes

TO DECORATE:
Lime wedges
Mint leaves

METHOD
1. Halve the limes, then squeeze.

2. Put the squeezed lime halves into a heatproof jug with the sugar and boiling water. Leave for 15 mins.

3. Add the salt. Stir and then strain it into a jug with the lime juice.

4. Add half a dozen ice cubes, cover and refrigerate for 2 hours or until chilled.

5. To serve, place two or three ice cubes in a glass and pour the limeade over them.

6. Add a lime wedge and a mint leaf to decorate.

Hills as green as emeralds
Cover the countryside
Lakes as blue as sapphires
Are Ireland's special pride
And rivers that shine like silver
Make Ireland look so fair -
But the friendliness of her people
Is the richest treasure there.

My Own Recipes

My Own Recipes